"A tour de force view of th children in Birmingham (to read this and take acti

C000264035

"This book is a shocking indictment of modern-day civic governance and the lack of authentic concern by MPs, councillors and a transient senior management about the hardships suffered by Birmingham's children and families.

"O'Hara's heartfelt narrative should shame those in authority to take action – this book's recommendations are not just concerned with morality, they also make great business sense."

Dr Peter Unwin
Principal Social Work Lecturer

"Challenging structural inequality isn't easy but complacency in the face of it is, particularly from those of us who live in relative comfort.

"This book and ABC's work is a reminder that many are not afforded this luxury. That poverty and inequality continue to blight the lives of far too many children while others reap the benefits of living in one of the world's richest countries. That those who sit at the top tables are not just there to further their own careers and preserve the status quo.

"It should prick the conscience of all senior leaders in Birmingham and beyond to do more to prevent future generations from being left behind."

Shahid Naqvi
Editor of *Professional Social Work* magazine

"There is no such thing as other people's children,[1] a point well made in this book."

Salma Mirza
Children's Home Senior Residential Support Worker

"In this book, Eddie provides a fascinating historical insight and social observation regarding Birmingham as a city but also develops the history and purposes of All Birmingham's Children (ABC) extremely well. The work undertaken by ABC has made a significant difference to so many, yet one question that is an underlying theme within the book is 'Why have childhood poverty and food banks in Birmingham become the new normal?'

"The book highlights that a generation of communities have enjoyed everything the UK post-war social contract and welfare state has had to offer: free education, health provision, housing, social care, unemployment benefit and assistance. Consequently, for so many children living in Birmingham 'these can be the best of times with great opportunities ahead'. However, as highlighted for 32-54% of children living in Birmingham 'these are unfortunately the worst of times'.

"The book is further concerned with the questions of how so many children remain in this desperate situation? It offers a well-argued analysis with clear suggestions on how this could be achieved asking Birmingham's leadership

---

1   A poignant phrase, often used by those who fight and advocate for the rights of refugee children, when countering some of the cruel comments made by some commentators in respect of children who tragically drown crossing our seas in the search for a safer and more peaceful life.

to create a better child-friendly city and community where other organisations will want to follow.

"Carefully assembled, the chapters are well developed, leading into the next, advancing the reader with some thought-provoking statistics, allowing you to gain a deeper insight into the diversity of children's lives and opportunities.

"Each chapter is written by an author who has terrific personal and professional knowledge of the systems that support but that can also hinder Birmingham's development, which allows for an accurate and honest representation of the city. This develops to offer clear and articulated suggestions on how to promote the best interests of all children living in Birmingham and the wider community."

John McGowan
General Secretary, Social Workers Union

"I was aware that this was not going to be a 'good read', despite my hope otherwise. To see so much valued hard work, all of which only wanted the lives of children to be better, not perfect or unrealistic, just better, and for this work and commitment to be so fully dismissed and isolated is a truly dreadful indictment of the leaders of Birmingham. They should be utterly ashamed of themselves. Eddie and his joyful wants for the children and families he has supported and worked with should have been embraced. Instead, the Prophet has not been recognised for who and what he represented. What a truly dreadful story this tells."

Sam Jones
Independent Children's Advocate
& Complaint Investigator

"There's no doubt that the government's austerity programme has hit Birmingham hard and has made meeting the needs of all its children that much more difficult, but local representatives, working with charities like ABC, can still make a difference. This book is a timely reminder of the unacceptable disparity in life-chances that blights the lives of so many of our children. It is a call to action. We can do better. We must do better."

David Hughes
Branch Officer, Birmingham UNISON (pc)

"We don't seem to have moved very far in terms of child poverty, do we? I remember being horrified by the difference in living standards between richer and poorer parts of our community in the late 1960s and we should have travelled far beyond that point in this century. If we don't create and support a child-friendly city, how can Birmingham grow and thrive as a place for families to live, to enjoy themselves and to help all our children and future generations to live happy and fulfilling lives and to contribute to their community?"

Jackie Warr
Parent, Birmingham resident and a retired Social Worker

"Eddie O'Hara and ABC's book is a tale of anger.

"Of anger at over 100,000 children in Birmingham living in poverty and more and more families becoming poorer.

"Of anger at a Government that has cut Birmingham City Council's budget by 60% since 2010, leading to a 73% cut on children's social services despite increasing need.

"Of anger at a Council that has seen its services dwindle and done little publicly to challenge it.

"Of anger at Councillors who refuse to engage with even answering the simplest of questions: What have you done to promote the best interests of children in Birmingham?

"Of anger at an employer more angry at those asking questions than at the shocking reality of the answers.

"O'Hara's book charts a small campaign by a small organisation that has big expectations for one of the youngest cities in Europe.

"That high expectations to challenging poverty and increasing life chances are seen as problematic by the very people you'd expect to want embrace these ideas tells you all you need to know about why we all need to campaign harder to stop services and support breaking when people need them most."

Doug Morgan
Birmingham National Education Union Activist (pc)

"This book is important reading for anyone wanting to make a change. Eddie's honesty is both a searing indictment of the current system and leaders, and an endearing call to arms. He has acknowledged his surprise and hurt at the petty vindictiveness and bureaucratic indifference he has faced. But he has not lost his enthusiasm for his mission to support ALL of Birmingham's children. It's an inspiring mission, and one that we should all get behind."

Salma Yaqoob
Health Professional & Community Activist

Birmingham's Children
A Tale of Two Cities

"The best of times for some children...
the worst of times for other children"

Eddie O'Hara, BEM

Matador
Unit E2 Airfield Business Park,
Harrison Road, Market Harborough,
Leicestershire. LE16 7UL
Tel: 0116 2792299
Email: books@troubador.co.uk
Web: www.troubador.co.uk/matador
Twitter: @matadorbooks

ISBN 978 1803132 310

British Library Cataloguing in Publication Data.
A catalogue record for this book is available from the British Library.

Printed and bound in the UK by TJ Books Limitd, Padstow, Cornwall
Typeset in 11pt Minion Pro by Troubador Publishing Ltd, Leicester, UK

All costs associated with the production, printing and
distribution of this book were met by the author.

Matador is an imprint of Troubador Publishing Ltd

This book was inspired by

A lovely first-time mum and her beautiful little flower boy

This book is dedicated to

All children living in Birmingham

ACKNOWLEDGEMENTS & THANKS

All trustees of All Birmingham's Children past and present: not least Caroline O'Hara and our three beautiful, albeit barmy, children and my three older brothers for their continued and unwavering support.

Jo Osmond (ABC Trustee and health manager), Niall McAuley (ABC Trustee and retired social worker), Liam O'Hara (ABC Deputy Chair and retired police detective), Michael Hall (social worker), Cheryl Hedges (ABC Trustee and retired lecturer), Steve Hedges (librarian), Nicky Pittaway (ABC Trustee and school safeguarding manager), Matiss Krumins (barrister), Penny Thompson (Chair Birmingham Local Safeguarding Children's Partnership), G.M., H.M., Helen Rees (senior nursing lecturer at University of Birmingham), Richard Chant (West Midlands Police youth officer), Alastair Gibbons (former Director of Birmingham Children's Trust), Dr Peter Unwin (head of social work department at Worcester University), Jack Wylie (web designer), Sam Jones (independent children's advocate & complaint investigator), Cailin Gallagher (photographer).

Minuteman Press (Hall Green), Myriad Consulting, 3PB Barristers Chamber, John Lewis Stores (Birmingham),

Greater Birmingham Chamber of Commerce, Kemps Publishing, Social Work Union, British Association of Social Workers, Social Work Action Network, Unison and National Education Union, National Children's Day UK, Tiger Lab Network c/o Birmingham City University Business Department, Birmingham Updates, Foyles Bookshop and Blue.Com Radio.

HRH Queen Elizabeth II for recognising the positive contribution which All Birmingham's Children Campaigning Charity has and continues to make to the lives of all children living in Birmingham, by honouring myself in this year's New Year's Honours List (2022) with a 'British Empire Medal' for Chairing All Birmingham's Children and continued 'Services to Children and Families'.

As the author of this book, I accept complete responsibility for all its contents. The opinions expressed within this book are mine and mine alone. Should there be any factual inaccuracies, I apologise unreservedly and ask that you kindly let me know so that they can be corrected in any future editions.

CONTENTS

FOREWORD

This book was born out of a brief conversation a few years ago which I (as a registered social worker) had with a first-time new mum.

One day, during quite a challenging period for this new mum, we were discussing the similar challenges faced by other parents in raising their children. Suffice to say, my new mum, who was understandably pre-occupied with the task of parenting and protecting her own child, informed me that at that moment in time, her sole concern was her own child and not the children of others.

This was not the first time I had heard this viewpoint and indeed I have on occasions in the past thought similar things with my own children. However, this conversation led me to begin thinking that even from a purely self-interested position, surely it is in everybody's interest to be concerned about other people's children. Not least because they or their own children will one day most likely be mixing with, growing up with, learning with, working with and having relationships with future adults. Furthermore, our children will grow to form the society we will live in and inherit the world we leave behind.

This brief encounter set in motion a process of thought which led me, and a handful of like-minded folks, to set up

'All Birmingham's Children (ABC)', a local campaigning charity to promote the best interests of all children living in Birmingham, on the basis that no child growing up in Birmingham could reach their full potential until all children living in Birmingham were afforded genuine equality of opportunities.

For several years now ABC volunteers have worked tirelessly to promote the best interests of all children living in Birmingham, using every opportunity we could to promote its message. We constantly explored and challenged those in power about why our city of nearly half a million (460,000) children, 461 schools, several world-class universities, magnificent hospitals… could also have 32-54%[2] of its children living in poverty, have the highest infant mortality rate and obesity rates in the UK and have witnessed a 500% increase in the use of food banks in recent years.

The then Director of Children's Social Care (Social Services) was very supportive of our campaigning work, and at the start of our campaign a senior Birmingham City Council Cabinet member even said: "Our children need ABC!"

As our message grew so too did our presence. Amongst others, in private a local surgeon and local family judge all asked to be kept informed of developments. This then led to one, now retired, local MP publicly supporting us and the CEO of the local chamber of commerce inviting us to present at their Chamber Exposition. Soon we were also invited to self-nominate for a community award (which we

---

2   32% is the city average with 54% being the highest in one of our 10 wards.

declined), a local printer sponsored our literature, one local radio promoted us, professional social work organisations and local teaching unions publicly supported us, and we had visits from national media in the UK and state media from Sweden and Japan... things were gathering apace!

We naively thought, living and working that in a city which has more children and young people than any other city in Europe, that our calls for the promotion of the best needs of all children would continue to be welcomed and promoted by all those with any interest in the city and all of its children. We hoped that ABC would provide an inspiration to other communities across the country.

How wrong we were! Despite ABC's many early successes, including growing local, national and international recognition, the increasing apathy, resistance and opposition from those with local and national power and influence across the city put paid to our initial progress which required us to stand back and consider how best continue our work.

This book is an illustration of why ABC's work has and continues to be vital in highlighting a route map for the next chapter in trying to make Birmingham a city that truly values and promotes the best interest of all its children.

INTRODUCTION[3]

I love Birmingham, I really do. My wife and I were both born and raised in Birmingham and now live less than a mile from where we spent our childhoods.

I love the fact that we have raised our family in Birmingham and still work in Birmingham. I love the fact that our children attended the same primary school that both my wife and I both attended, and that my wife and I both attended the same secondary school as my mum attended in the 1940s!

---

3   Birmingham's first official community flag. The flag was designed in 2015 by two 10-year-old local boys, Thomas Keogh and David Smith. The blue zigzag represents the B from the name Birmingham and the local canals. The gold zigzag represents the closed lock gates on the canals, and the Roman M represents the number 1000 to reflect Birmingham as the city of a 1000 trades, and finally the bull represents the Bull Ring.

I love the fact that I went to primary school with our local postman and my old school friends still manage the local supermarket, the local jewellers and local pizza restaurant.

I love the feeling of living within a changing community and that our children have grown up and benefited from a wonderful multi-cultural upbringing and education.

I love the fact that as a family we have all benefited from wonderful schools, local authority music services, leisure services, parks services, youth services, swimming pools, Sunday league football, further education colleges, local universities and colleges.

I love the fact that my wife, myself and my three brothers have all worked as public servants in Birmingham to try and improve the lives of others.

I love 'Brummies'… most of them are without doubt the salt of the earth!

Yes, I love Birmingham, I really do.

However, for far too many local children today (32-54%) sadly there is not much to love about living in Birmingham.

This book will look at why for many children living in Birmingham **'these are the best of times'**[4] when at the same time, for 32-54% of children living in Birmingham **'these are the worst of times'**.[5]

---

4   Charles Dickens: *A Tale of Two Cities* (1859).
5   Charles Dickens was a great friend of Birmingham and was the 16th President of the Birmingham and Midland Institute. He marvelled at the use of gas electric lighting in 1793 in Soho Foundry. His first public reading of *A Christmas Carol* was performed outside Birmingham Town Hall in 1853. Indeed, not only was the reading room in the Birmingham Midland Institute named after him, but the adjoining road which runs through the heart of the city was renamed Great Charles Street.

This book will set out the cold facts of why in a city of 1.2 million people, including nearly half a million children and young people, with 461 schools, 6 internationally acclaimed universities, a world-class medical school, law schools, magnificent museums, wonderful art, conservatoire, international symphony hall, international convention centres and soon to be hosts of the 2022 Commonwealth Games, we still have 32-54% of our own children living in poverty[6] and have 3 out of 10 of the UK's poorest neighbourhoods.

Why, in England's 'second city' of 1000 trades, where billions of pounds are being invested by multi-national companies, with world-class teaching hospitals, do we still have the highest infant mortality and infant obesity rates in the UK?

Why, despite the fact that our city was founded and developed by great visionaries such as Chamberlain, Boulton, Cadbury and Watt, who promoted public interest and well-being… are our public services now in relative decay and failing many of our children?

Why, in a city which has 10 Members of Parliament, 100 Local Councillors, and 1 Regional Mayor, do most elected officials continue to allow these inequalities to persist?

Why, when so many of our local business do so much for our community (so much of their good work is not known about), do others fail to recognise the mutual benefit and great wealth of local young talent, which will ensure their future prosperity and that of our city by offering low-paid and insecure employment?

---

6   Poverty is officially determined as living on 60% below the median household income after housing costs.

We will examine why the patchwork of local initiatives, charitable projects and statutory services have gaping holes through which so many children fall.

We will explore why so many otherwise decent people are content living with an existing system which is so firmly based on and rooted in inequality that is ruining the lives of 100,000s of our children every day. It will draw out some of the pitiful justifications made by community leaders which suggest that they believe it's 'always somebody else's responsibility' to improve the lives of children.

We will look at why so many of our publicly elected community leaders regard it as a personal affront when you ask them (as our publicly elected officials) to explain what they are proactively doing to promote the best interests of all children in their constituency, let alone across the whole city. We will also look at how this defensive approach and entrenched political mindset stifles local debate and negatively impacts on our children.

Finally, but most importantly, we will look at what can be done to genuinely move Birmingham forward in becoming the great city it could be if only it could use its political and business power to promote the best interests of all its citizens, especially its fast-growing population of nearly half a million children and young people.

BIRMINGHAM: A CITY OF 1000 TRADES[7]

Birmingham's origins began as a hamlet around the River Rea in the neighbourhood we now know as Digbeth about 1500 years ago and received its Royal Charter Mark in 1166.

By the 18th century, at the peak of the industrial revolution, Birmingham had become the workshop of the world, famed for being a city of 1000 trades.

As an industrial city with a surging population Birmingham's future was very much shaped by civic investment, a growing canal transport network, scientific achievement, commercial innovation, public virtue and having a reputation of not being controlled by government dictat and restrictive guilds, all of which helped bring about major social and economic reforms.

---

7 (No city can claim to be a great city when between 32-54% of its children are poor.)

Birmingham was well on its way to fast becoming a great city with visionary leaders.

In 1832 Birmingham was given its first opportunity to elect its own Members of Parliament and later in 1873 went on to elect Joseph Chamberlain as its first Mayor.

Since the time of the first world war Birmingham has been regarded as Britain's Second City[8] on the basis of the population living within its boundaries.

CURRENT FACTS, FIGURES AND CHALLENGES:

Whilst it is very tempting to spend pages analysing figures and statistics about the history and political demography of Birmingham, to do so might actually have the effect of distracting from the central message of this book, which is to look forward.

Suffice to say, should you be interested in this detail, central government and Birmingham City Council both have archives, which describe and quantify the perilous state of our local affairs in terms of provision of services for children and young people.

For our purposes of the message within this book we know the following:

Birmingham has a population of approximately 1,200,000 citizens, of which approximately 460,000 are children, and 461 schools.

---

8   'Birmingham is Britain's second city, it is a powerhouse', David Cameron (ex-prime minister), *Birmingham Post,* 13-2-15.

At a time when Birmingham's population is growing our local government grant from central government has been consistently cut (60% over the last 10 years alone) year after year for the last decade at least… leaving us with very few resources in the public purse.

In 2010 Birmingham City Council spent £584[9] million on Children's Social Care. In 2021 Birmingham City Council (via the Children's Trust) spent £203 million on Children's Social Care. When one then allows for 27% inflation over the same period,[10] this is a massive 73% cut in spending on the most vulnerable children in our city.

Over the last 30 years we have also seen nationally the dismantling, privatisation and closure of much of the public services we once took for granted, such as: Sure Start, children centres, youth clubs, libraries, leisure facilities, swimming pools, parks, local social services, neighbourhood offices, community police stations and neighbourhood police officers, health centres, etc.

As with most British cities and towns, it has been the eastern wards of Birmingham which have taken the biggest brunt of these cuts, because these areas tend to be the most economically deprived. This phenomenon being down to no other fact than historically, the well-heeled have often opted to live in the west side of cities and towns to escape the prevailing westerly winds blowing the urban smog and smoke over them.

Presently 32-54% of Birmingham's children live below the poverty line and rely on the growing number of food

---

9   Birmingham City Council Budget Archives.
10   Bank of England official inflationary figures 2010-2021.

banks and charitable organisations across the city. It seems food banks have now become the new norm.

Birmingham has approximately 2000 children who are looked after (otherwise known as being in care) by the local authority (this is 0.43% of children living in the city), with a further 1,2000 cases open to Birmingham Children's Trust (2.6% of children living in the city).

The last statistics quoted by a Freedom of Information request (October 2021) disclosed that in Birmingham 116,552 children are living in poverty.

This means that less than 2% of Birmingham children living in poverty receive any additional support or input from Birmingham's Children's Trust, which is after all the statutory body accountable to Birmingham City Council to assess and meet the needs of children who are regarded as being Children in Need.[11] This is despite Section 17 of the Children Act placing a clear duty on local authorities to assess and respond to any child believed to be in need.

We have a Children's Trust which, despite being staffed by some fantastic social workers, allied professional and support staff, spends most of its time firefighting for children most in need, whilst simultaneously trying to meet unachievable and unrealistic Ofsted targets.

It is therefore a huge mistake for anyone, particularly our elected leaders, to think that Birmingham Children's Trust has the political remit, resources or ability to respond to all of the children living in Birmingham who are in dire need of support.

The reality is that most of our local children who are living in poverty and need of support never get anywhere

---

11   Defined by Section 17 of the Children Act 1989.

near, let alone receive help or support from, Birmingham's Children's Trust.

Out of the 10 Birmingham wards:

1. Ladywood ward has 54.5% of children living in poverty.
2. Hall Green ward has 54.3% of children living in poverty.
3. Hodge Hill ward has 52% of children living in poverty.

These 3 wards are in the UK's top 10 most deprived neighbourhoods.

One cannot ignore, however, that in the more affluent, less socially deprived area of Sutton Coldfield, there are still 3401 children registered as living in poverty.

In October 2021[12] Birmingham had 6537 children registered as being homeless with 6325 living in temporary accommodation, of which 2478 are living in private temporary accommodation.

Preet Gill (MP for Edgbaston) noted in May 2021 that childhood poverty in Birmingham is a 'National Shame'.[13]

Birmingham has one of if not the highest obesity rates in children moving on from primary school in England and this situation has not changed in over a decade (41%).[14] Birmingham also has one if not the highest infant mortality rates in England.[15]

---

12   Freedom of Information Request, August 2021.
13   Birmingham Live Updates, 21-5-21.
14   Birmingham Update, 15-10-18.
15   BBC News, 21-4-21.

Birmingham no longer owns any of its children's residential homes; these are now owned and operated by 19 private landlord companies. This situation is made even worse for many older children, who are being placed by the local authority into accommodation which is neither regulated nor inspected by the local council, Ofsted or CQC.

Clearly Birmingham is a tale of two cities: whilst poverty in Birmingham is growing, the city is also becoming richer every year by virtue of the polarisation of wealth and new incoming investment.

We cannot ignore the direct impact that this polarisation is having on our children. Wherever you live in Birmingham poverty affects children.

BIRMINGHAM'S CHILDREN: THE BEST OF TIMES

For many children in Birmingham who have access to resources and money… notwithstanding the impact of Covid and exceptions, they may have the privilege of experiencing **'the best of times'**.

After all, Birmingham boasts:

- Some of the best public schools in the UK which provide magnificent extracurricular opportunities and cultural facilities.
- Private medical care which provides a range of bespoke private clinics and hospitals.
- High-tech STEM (Science Technology Engineering Maths) facilities.
- World-class cultural institutions, international sporting facilities, a school's music service (now a Trust), a world-class symphony hall, theatres, science museum and health clubs, spas, etc.
- Access to great sporting events, test cricket, international rugby and football, the 2022 Commonwealth Games, etc.
- Access to a range of beautiful well-kitted-out gyms,

health clubs, a number of private parks, a beautiful botanical garden, country clubs.

- Access to an international airport, HS2 and being at the centre of the UK motorway hub.

It goes without saying that children who have access to the best that Birmingham can provide are more likely to:

- Enjoy more family downtime as a family and go on the odd holiday.
- Have a secure family home, where they will not have to worry about food, heating or being evicted any day.
- Live within a family who are cash and / or time rich.
- Live without the fear of exploitation, toxic stress, violence, mental health issues, domestic abuse, substance misuse issues, etc.
- Look forward to exploring what higher education might offer without having to worry about the mountains of debt which awaits them.
- Look forward to the future and all the joys and adventures it will bring.

BIRMINGHAM'S CHILDREN: THESE ARE THE WORST OF TIMES

Conversely, for the rest (up to 32-54% of children living in poverty in at least 3 parts of the city) and many 10,000s more children across the city living in poverty, **'these are the worst of times'**.

- They are less likely to survive infancy.
- They are more likely to experience obesity by the age of 16 and general poorer health.
- More likely to go to bed each night hungry and suffering the physical pain and psychological damage which hunger brings.
- Less chance of experiencing any early intervention or socialisation in pre-school services.
- Attend an under-resourced school.
- The indignity and embarrassment of going to school wearing old, ill-fitting and dirty clothes as opposed to a clean, non-stigmatising uniform.
- Standing in a food bank queue with their parents or carers.
- Being unrecognised and unsupported carers for members of their own family.
- Having much-reduced life / employment opportunities.

- A reluctance to explore higher education because of the mountains of debt which will follow.
- Fewer opportunities to access libraries as they close across the city, with a negative impact on education.
- Less access to free leisure activities as many of these services are now closed or run by private firms, having a negative impact on health and wellbeing.
- Less opportunities to take up an instrument or carry on with it because to do so, the vast majority of children require additional (private) lessons.
- Less opportunity to access our great pay-to-enter Science Museum or Millennium Point facilities, with a negative impact on education.
- The increased likelihood of exploitation by gangs and sub-cultures which prey on young people who are disaffected / alienated from the cultural activity they see all around them but cannot afford to access.
- Less likely to access mental health services when needed.
- No childhood hope or excitement about what the future as an adult might bring.
- The list goes on and on and on.

The collective impact of all of the above is that for many of our children their future will be hugely limited and negatively affected in terms of education, health and well-being, job opportunities, which in turn will affect their children and the future well-being of our city.

ALL BIRMINGHAM'S CHILDREN ABC

CAMPAIGNING CHARITY:[16] ITS ORIGINS, EARLY DAYS, SUCCESSES, POLITICAL RESISTANCE & LESSONS LEARNT!

All Birmingham's Children set about forging a campaign to promote the best interest of all children living (and visiting) Birmingham. ABC was founded a few years ago following a simple everyday conversation I had with a parent about the challenges of raising her child.

As referred to previously the conversation in brief raised the issue of how can we as a community ensure the best for our own children without simultaneously being concerned about other children? After all, our own children will grow up with, play, work and go on to form relationships with other children.

Surely therefore it is in the best interest of us all to be concerned about the lives of other children and do what we can to promote their best interests as well?

---

16   All Birmingham's Children is a non-registered charity on the basis that its income is less than £5000. In fact, its current bank balance is less than £0!

Suffice to say, I thought about this relatively straightforward question for several months and pondered about why, as a community in Birmingham (and elsewhere), we often see the fortunes and futures of our own children and the children of others as being somehow separate from each other? How have we as a community come to see it almost as normal that there exists such levels of poverty, inequality and despair between different groups of children? Why does this not repulse us and motivate us all to collectively do something about it?

Why is it that despite the continued cuts by national government to local authority funding and public services,[17] some 60% in the last 10 years, a policy which has been going on for over 30 years by successive governments and exacerbated by the recent policies of austerity and centralisation, we as a community appear to show very little resistance to the devasting effects this is having on a significant section of our community, not least the everyday lives of so many children? When did childhood poverty and food banks in Birmingham become the new normal?

Perhaps we have collective amnesia about the gains in the past or feel that equality of opportunity is a great idea which is only worth fighting for when it affects our lives and the lives of our children.

How many single-issue campaigns have you seen where people only initiate or become involved in an issue when the issue directly affects them?

An example of a local single issue was when one of our local MPs delivered her own child to Downing Street in

---

17   60% over the last 10 years alone: IFS.

protest against the impact on school hours due to increasing teachers' workloads. Despite this being an important issue, which has been alive for years, it seems that this issue only became important to the MP when it affected their child, despite it being important to many 1000s of other less fortunate parents in their constituency for years.

With the above in mind, I wrote to the then Children's Commissioner[18] asking what her office and the government in general had in terms of a national policy designed to promote the best interests of all children, particularly those children living in Birmingham.

The response from the office of the Children's Commissioner (England) was that as a national body it did not involve itself directly in the detail of local provision of services to children services.

As a result of the response from the Children's Commissioner, I then wrote to the leader of Birmingham City Council and asked what citywide policy we had to promote the best interests of all children living in Birmingham.

Birmingham City Council informed me that we, as a city of nearly half a million children and young people, did not have such a plan. Instead, the City Council's focus was primarily on providing the minimum statutory services to children it was obliged to as part of government-determined local statutory services.[19]

It therefore quickly became apparent that I needed a plan, our children needed a plan, and our city needed a plan... a plan that was not just for disabled, male, female,

---

18   Anne Longfield.
19   Which, as noted by continuous and countless government (Ofsted, CQC, etc.) reports, they consistently fail to do.

poorly, black, white, able-bodied, gay, religious, non-religious children, etc., but for ALL children living in Birmingham. If you were under the age of 18 then you mattered to us!

It was time to start All Birmingham's Children campaigning charity (ABC)![20]

Over the next few weeks, I enlisted the help of a number of local people involved with children,[21] most of whom had worked with all types / ages of children across the city for between 15-30 years each and many were also experienced parents of children who were growing / had grown up in Birmingham.

ABC volunteers provided the campaign with insight, experience and ambition to move forward in addressing how to promote the best interests of all children living in Birmingham.

I also informed my then boss and the (then) Director of Birmingham Children's Social Care of my intentions and spoke with a couple of local councillors.

We agreed that as my activities with ABC would be voluntary and completely separate from my role as a citywide senior manager in Birmingham's Children's Social Care / Trust, that any questions / queries / complaints about ABC from local politicians should be relayed to me directly to deal with.

---

20 ABC has always been a non-registered charity simply on the grounds that its income has never exceeded £5000.

21 Social workers, teachers, police, health workers, students, businesspeople and lawyers. Between us we had over 200+ years of local experience of caring for, working with, educating and nurturing children.

This was a simple task: after all, who could refuse to help a campaigning charity promoting the best interest of all children living in Birmingham?

During the summer of 2018 ABC began in earnest planning what we hoped to achieve and how we would set about it.

To begin with ABC were very fortunate to have the backing of three major supporters:

1. Hall Green Minute Man Printing: a local family-run printing firm who chose ABC as their charity of the coming year and went on to provide us with untold amounts of media advice, leaflets, campaigning material, etc.
2. Myriad Consulting: a local IT / Financial firm who provided us with someone to set up a website / Twitter / LinkedIn, etc.
3. Two former employees of Birmingham Children's Social Services who kindly provided ABC with cash donations (£300) that helped us set up a bank account.

During the summer of 2018 we also began providing regular emails to all 100 councillors, 10 MPs and 1 Regional Mayor, outlining to them who we were and what we were seeking to achieve.

I also met with the Chair of the Birmingham Local Safeguarding Children Board, who kindly provided ABC with some useful networking ideas and useful contacts to follow up; one of these contacts was Councillor Jayne Francis, who was then the Chair of the Education and Skills Committee.

4-9-18: ABC met with Councillor Francis. This was a very important first meeting with anyone from Birmingham

City Council because it enabled us to set out why we felt the need to set up ABC and what its initial vision was.

During this meeting we also raised the prospect of Birmingham City Council adopting the much-heralded and acclaimed Preston Model of local authorities procuring local services for the benefit of all local citizens, not least for the benefit of all local children. In brief, it is a model of local government which is built on a belief and commitment to local people by taking back control of their economy and community and creates local reinvestment of wealth.[22]

It was made very clear at this meeting that ABC were absolutely committed to working with and supporting Birmingham City Council wherever possible in promoting the needs of all children living in Birmingham. However, ABC were also committed to challenging and holding Birmingham City Council (via our Positive Action Reports[23]) to account.

After this meeting Jayne Francis (Chair of Education & Skills Committee) went on to tweet:

"Our children need ABC!"

During the summer of 2018 ABC also contacted and met with the founders of National Children's Day UK[24]

---

22 Preston Model: www.preston.gov.uk/article/1339/What-is-Preston-Model-

23 Positive Action Reports were ABC bi-annual reports setting out explicitly all elected representatives' responses to 2 questions: what have you done in the last 6 months to explicitly promote the best interest, of all children living in Birmingham? What do you intend on doing in the next 6 months to explicitly promote the best interests of all children living in Birmingham?

24 www.nationalchildrensdayuk.com

(NCDUK), which is a national campaign set up to promote the annual celebration of a National Children's Day within communities across the UK. The purpose of this was to seek help and advice about how we might begin such community celebrations here in Birmingham. Suffice to say NCDUK have been incredibly positive and supportive to ABC since it was formed.

Later that year we met with two of the founders of NCDUK,[25] who kindly made a special trip to Birmingham to meet with us. Throughout 2018-2019 NCDUK were a tremendous source of help, support and inspiration to ABC and kindly went on to tweet:

"ABC a small charity with a big heart"

26-9-18, ABC had its first formal planning meeting.

The sense of excitement at our first meeting was made all the more palpable due to the fact that the High Sheriff of Birmingham[26] had accepted an invitation to attend our first ever formal meeting. As an experienced local dignitary, the attendance of the High Sheriff alone gave us much to think about in terms of how we focused our campaign. Unfortunately, the new CEO of Birmingham Children's Trust sent their apologies.

Following our inaugural planning meeting ABC drew up and agreed its mission statement:

---

25 One of whom is the nationally acclaimed children's author Sally Grindley.

26 Chris Loughton.

<u>ABC 1st Mission Statement & 10 Objectives</u>

To encourage EVERYONE living and working
in Birmingham to help make our city the best & safest
place for ALL children to grow up in by actively
campaigning for the following 10 objectives.

THE 10 OBJECTIVES:

1. Encourage Birmingham City Council and Birmingham Businesses to organise and celebrate National Children's Day each year in May.
2. Encourage all elected Birmingham politicians, community and business leaders to actively and explicitly promote the needs of ABC. (We will produce and publish a bi-annual Positive Action report highlighting what each local politician has done in the last 6 months and what they will be doing in the next 6 months to promote the best interests of all local children.)
3. For ABC to be actively engaged in developing, reviewing and implementing this campaign.
4. For ABC to live and grow up in a city free from the fear of crime and domestic abuse.
5. For ABC to have access to decent housing, 'good' education and quality employment / training opportunities.
6. For ABC to have FREE / REDUCED cost access to youth and leisure services.
7. For ABC to have FREE / REDUCED cost public transport. If London (younger) children have FREE

bus, train and Tube travel, then why can't Birmingham children have FREE access to all public transport?

8. For ABC to have timely access to high-quality physical and mental health care.

9. For all local faith organisations to work together for the best interest of ABC regardless of faith / non-faith.

10. For all local businesses to pledge support for ABC. Our aim was to get 250 local business signed up by 2022.

WE WILL DO THIS BY:

- Positively supporting, making formal and informal links, and constructively challenging local politicians, agencies and businesses.
- Celebrating, recognising and publishing all positive contributions which reflect some / all of the above objectives.

27-9-18 The Director of Birmingham's Children's Trust (formerly Birmingham Children's Social Care) retired; however he very kindly continued to offer ABC support and advice.

November 2018: In amongst the usual frantic activity of ABC volunteers getting leaflets distributed citywide to libraries, schools, hospitals, etc., two other important events happened this month. The first was that Compass Events[27] had very kindly agreed that ABC could run a seminar at its forthcoming regional jobs fayre to be held in Birmingham on 4-3-19.

---

27   www.compassjobsfair.com

This was to be a great opportunity where ABC could highlight what was happening in Birmingham and discuss with and learn from others across the country about the importance of grassroots local community social work.

The second other important event this month was that after a local court hearing (at that point I was still working for Birmingham Children's Trust), one of our local senior family judges asked to speak with me privately about ABC.

Suffice to say, the judge was very impressed with what ABC was trying to achieve and assured me that where possible they would do whatever they could to support our aims.

December 2018: ABC met with the Regional Director of the Children's Society. Not only was this meeting an important aspect of networking, but it also provided a really useful and candid insight into how to navigate the inter-charity politics operating in Birmingham and further afield, not least how the competitive funding system discourages charities from working together when they have to compete separately for funding. The meeting was also an invaluable lesson in understanding who was involved in developing an emerging strategic children's plan. More about the city's strategic children's plan later.

January 2019: ABC's big launch; during this month we issued press releases and leaflets to all 100 elected Birmingham Councillors, 10 Birmingham MPs, 1 Regional Mayor, all local faith groups and youth organisations, all statutory services and local and national media. As one councillor later told us, if we had achieved nothing else, we had at least ensured that everyone in Birmingham Council House had heard of us!

February 2019: This month was a month of ups and downs! It began with a positive front page spread and editorial in *Professional Social Work* monthly magazine, highlighting our work and aims. The theme of the launch was that… 'it costs nothing to make a big difference'. Shahid Naviq (Editor of *PSW*) noted:

> "As an example of social work activism
> [ABC] is hard to beat"[28]

As the Chair of Birmingham and Solihull branch of the British Association of Social Workers (BASW), this month I also submitted a motion to support the work of ABC and encourage and support other similar initiatives across the UK. This motion was unanimously passed and went on to to be seconded by both the Worcester and Black Country branches of BASW. The England Committee of BASW agreed that our motion should go straight to the next UK Annual Conference, which was being held in Belfast on 21-6-19. As will be referred to later, our motion to support children across the UK was unanimously passed at the national conference in Belfast.

During February I also met with a senior matron / sister in Birmingham's Children's Hospital, who kindly listened to what I had to say about ABC and informed me of some of the staggering figures about local child infant mortality and childhood obesity.

As advised by a senior leader in the charity sector, this month I also met with an adviser from the National Lottery.

---

28   Shahid Naviq, Editor of *Professional Social Work*, Front Cover Feature Piece, May 2019.

In brief the adviser informed me that that because ABC's brief was so wide, and we could not provide specific details about how many and what type of child would benefit from our work, we would not be eligible for any local lottery funding. Thank heaven for volunteers!

Unfortunately, this month was also the month when we first encountered the start of serious local political resistance to what ABC was trying to achieve. Sadly, the first signs of overt resistance came in the shape of Birmingham Children's Trust.

Suffice to say, Birmingham Children's Trust (BCT), who were the main sponsors of the Compass Jobs Fayre due next month, had asked Compass to rescind their offer to ABC of doing a seminar on the theme of 'Community Social Work', as it might confuse delegates to the conference that the newly launched and statutorily funded Birmingham Children's Trust, which replaced Birmingham Children's Social Care, and ABC, which ran on a shoestring and the goodwill of a few local volunteers, were one and the same thing!

Anxious not to put our colleagues at Compass in any more of an awkward and embarrassing position than they were already finding themselves in, we reluctantly agreed to withdraw from the Compass Jobs Fayre.

Following the debacle over the Compass Jobs Fayre, I was then asked in my professional role as a citywide senior manager (court work and specialist assessments) in Birmingham Children's Trust (BCT) to attend the Birmingham Children's Trust Executive Board on 21-2-19 to discuss my ongoing role within ABC. This request did not come as a surprise, even though I had previously informed my manager (an Assistant Director), the recently retired Director of Birmingham Children's Social Care and the new

Chief Executive Officer of the newly formed Birmingham Children's Trust, of my involvement in ABC.

By the time of the meeting with the Birmingham Children's Trust Executive Board, I had taken the decision to temporarily step down as Chair of ABC to prevent any confusion and possible perceived conflicts. I also restated that ABC's work was separate to Birmingham Children's Trust's statutory provision of selected services. That said, during the meeting the Executive Board requested that I sign a statement of 'No Conflict' and that all future questions about my role within ABC would only be discussed at directorate board level and not by my line manager (who was an assistant director).

In the event, I was never provided with a 'No Conflict' statement to sign and the following month, after working on and off for Birmingham Social Service for nearly 30 years with an unblemished work record, the Birmingham Children's Trust Executive Board made my post (and by definition me) redundant, replacing my job with three lower-grade posts.

The pressure was building and clearly 'they', whoever 'they' were, did not like ABC challenging the status quo within the city on what 'they' were and were not doing to promote the best interest of all children.

March 2019 began by ABC once again writing to Birmingham City Council Chief Executive Officer (who like many before her has since resigned to take on other higher-paid roles) to seek contact and discussion about our aims. However, this attempt and every other attempt since, to contact whoever was / is the current Birmingham City Council Chief Executive Officer, has always failed to result in an acknowledgment of our contact, let alone an offer of a meeting.

4-3-19: As ABC were no longer welcome inside at the Compass Jobs Fayre, ABC volunteers[29] met outside the conference centre on a public path and began leafleting delegates with information about the work ABC was doing as they arrived. ABC volunteers were then asked by conference security to stop handing out any further information about ABC. The ABC volunteers duly agreed and left.

3 days later (7-3-19) Birmingham Children's Trust Executive made my post redundant. I was informed of this verbally on 22-3-19.

On the bright side, March 2019 also brought a number of positive steps forward. Roger Godsiff (MP) agreed to meet with us and went on to offer his public support for the work of ABC. As referred to later, Roger Godsiff was the only one of Birmingham's 10 MPs we are aware of that has ever publicly supported ABC's work.

A few days later I also met with Councillor Kate Booth (former BCC Cabinet Lead for Children's Services), who kindly agreed to re-circulate our guidance to councillors on how they might proactively support the best interests of all children living in Birmingham, not just those children living in their own constituencies. Councillor Kate Booth went on to provide public support for our call for a National Children's Day and very kindly turned up with Cllr Lou Robson to (19-5-19) to offer their support on the day.

This month I also met with the Chief Executive Officer of the Greater Birmingham Chamber of Commerce (GBCC), who kindly invited ABC to attend the next Greater Birmingham Chamber of Common Exposition at Edgbaston

---

29   I was not present.

Cricket Ground. This event in itself proved to be a great success and confirmed beyond all doubt that local businesses[30] were keen and eager to support the idea of promoting the best interest of all local children living in Birmingham. Of the dozens of conversations we had (including a speed networking event), not one local representative from the West Midlands appeared unresponsive to the work of ABC.

Furthermore, as a result of attending the GBCC Expo, Jill Middleton from Birmingham City University Business Development Team (Tiger Lab) kindly nominated ABC for a community award of £250 (funded by Birmingham Updates) which we went on to win the following month! Every penny of the £250 was spent on gifts to give out at May's National Children's Day celebrations.

April 2019 saw the start of a project where ABC began presenting awards[31] to organisations who had demonstrated that they were trying to support the best interest of all children living in Birmingham.

---

30   Birmingham has 40,000 local businesses.
31   These plaques were often provided for us free by Hall Green Minute Man Printers.

Word was spreading about our work and in April 2019 ABC were invited to the Social Work Action Network (SWAN) conference in Liverpool. Again, this was a great opportunity to spread the word of what we are doing and what's more whilst we were in Liverpool the Social Work Union (SWU) kindly donated a further £250 to our campaign. Every penny of the £250 was spent on gifts to give out at May's National Children's Day celebrations.

May 2019 was a great month; it began with an article on ABC in the Social Workers Union newsletter, a productive meeting with the West Midlands Regional Co-op Director (food), being interviewed by FREE Radio and also continued to get plugs by Birmingham's Bluedot Radio station.[32]

The icing on the cake though came in June when ABC organised and held Birmingham's 1st ever National Children's Day on 1-5-19. This event was publicly supported by 3 local councillors, John Lewis Partnership, Foyles Bookshop, The Works, Hall Green Minuteman Press, etc.

After the success of Birmingham's 1st ever National Children's Day celebrations in 2019, we carefully planned to make the 2020 celebration even bigger and more inclusive. NCDUK were very keen to showcase Birmingham as an example to other communities across the UK.

June 2019: With our petition in hand from the National Children's Day, ABC started to formally call upon Birmingham City Council to proactively work towards making Birmingham into a 'Child-Friendly City'.

ABC also travelled to the Titanic Conference Centre in Belfast to the BASW Annual Conference, which was

---

32 www.bluedotradio.com

being held, to push Birmingham and Solihull Branch's motion in support of ABC's work and similar initiatives across the UK. With the additional seconding support and inspiring speech on our behalf from Dr Peter Unwin from the Worcester Branch, our motion was passed unanimously and became part of BASW national conference plan.

Whilst we were in Belfast, we also presented our hosts with their own local ABC Banner, All Belfast Children! The point of this being simply that we were trying to model our own approach for others to see, consider and perhaps take forward their own local variation with appropriate support and advice from ABC if needed.

That month I also met with a local University Director. The subject of the meeting was to look at how Birmingham city centre universities, colleges and museums could host / facilitate future National Children's Day celebrations / festivals. The idea made perfect sense as all of the universities / institutions were situated side by side in the city centre and provided lots of child-friendly areas inside and out. Who could possibly object? See overleaf!

All Belfasts Children

A campaign to promote the best interests of All Belfast's Children

It costs nothing to make a big difference

www.allbelfastschildren.com

In July 2019 ABC published its first Positive Action Report. Sadly, out of a potential 111 elected Cllrs, MPs and Regional Mayor who were asked to participate... only one elected leader, Cllr Kerry Jenkins, did so. This lack of active political engagement is something which will be explored later within this book.

Also in July, we were invited to meet with the Chief Executive Officer of the NHS Clinical Commissioning Group, who was keen to understand what ABC was all about. This was a very positive meeting and the CEO agreed to do what he could to support the wider aims of ABC.

Later that month we also met with the West Midlands Police Youth Officers, who have continued to provide ABC with useful advice and contacts.

On the personal recommendation of the CEO of the Greater Birmingham Chamber of Commerce, we also managed to secure a meeting with the owner of one of the main digital roadside advertisers in the region. The aim of this was to see if they would be willing to donate 5-30 seconds a day on their advertising boards to float some adverts around the city wishing for example all children living in Birmingham a 'Happy Holiday', 'Good luck with their exams', Happy Xmas, Eid, Hanukkah, etc. Whilst this was a productive awareness-raising meeting and an opportunity to plant a few seeds for the future, we never made any actual headway in terms of any cost-free options from the agency.

August 2019 was spent preparing for attending a Unison Friendship Festival which Donald McCombie (Unison Education Officer) kindly invited us to.

September 2019 continued to provide some positive

steps forward before what can only be described as a car crash meeting!

More about the positives first: this month we were visited by colleagues from Sweden who were keen to know about our campaign and went on to publish a positive article about our work. Interestingly, after a comprehensive walking tour of the city our Swedish colleagues were startled by what they regarded was the obvious lack of child play facilities within the city-centre areas for young families.

This month I also met with Helen Rees (Senior Nursing Lecturer at University of Birmingham Medical School). Helen had been a longstanding supporter of what ABC was trying to achieve and invited me to speak with 140 student health visitors about the importance of community involvement in the development of all children. This meeting was also an opportunity to explore the issue of a developing a Birmingham Child Passport for all children born in Birmingham or coming to live here. More about this later.

23-9-19: National Children's Day 2020 Planning Meeting Car Crash! After a year of building awareness and support across the city for future National Children's Day celebrations in Birmingham we had managed to convene an 'Ideas Meeting' of key partners to discuss possible future options / potential for a National Children's Day party / festival. Invitations had been sent, agendas, leaflets and desk / floor banners had been kindly produced and provided free by Minute Man Hall Green.

The meeting was hosted by one of the local city centre universities and attended by senior and junior representatives from the local universities, Birmingham City

Council, Birmingham Children's Trust, Greater Birmingham Chamber of Commerce, West Midlands Police, NHS Clinical Commissioning Group, etc.

Social Workers Union, British Association of Social Workers, National Education Union, UNISON and National Children's Day UK all sent their warm wishes and support.

Suffice to say, despite the positive messages and ambitions being discussed and promoted within the meeting, two junior representatives from different organisations appeared to be intent on finding fault and obstacles to almost every idea and suggestion put forward and added nothing positive to the discussion other than to focus on what they and their own particular agencies might get out of it or be risking in terms of reputational damage.

It cannot be underestimated just how destructive their presence was at such an important meeting and the negative impact it had on partners willing to take a leap of faith and work in partnership, which was so key to the success of achieving any kind of forward motion.

At a subsequent National Children's Day planning meeting a few months later, many of the key partners did not attend and the momentum was clearly faltering. At that meeting we decided to review how we might take the idea of celebrating a National Children's Day forward.

October 2019: we were also visited by members of the Japanese Press (Ashanti Press), who, like our colleagues from Sweden, were keen to visit Birmingham and hear about our campaign. Once again, we took them for a walking tour of the city centre and spoke about Birmingham as a whole. Unsurprisingly, they too noted the lack of a child-friendly feel to the city centre and surrounding areas.

Also, in October 2019 ABC had a stand at the Greater Birmingham Chamber of Commerce Autumn Exposition at Aston Villa football ground and *Chamber Link* magazine ran a very positive editorial piece on what ABC were trying to achieve across the city.

December 2019 saw ABC placing adverts across Birmingham wishing all children living in Birmingham a Merry Xmas and a Happy New Year.

2020 brought increasing political criticism from a few local councillors accusing our campaign of being 'reprehensible', 'presumptuous' and 'uncaring'.

One of the most senior members of the councillor's leadership team claimed that ABC was accusing them of not caring or promoting the best interests of all children living in Birmingham and because of this they found it difficult to engage with ABC or our 'cause', if that is what we thought.

That one of the most senior councillors should respond to the issue of the best interests of all children in Birmingham somehow as a 'cause', and not their legal and moral duty, explains better than I can, why in many ways Birmingham City Council continues to fail great swathes of its children and young people.

January 2020: In an effort to break what appeared to be a growing impasse with our elected representatives, ABC contacted every one of our 100 Councillors, 10 MPs and regional Mayor and suggested that it might be beneficial to all of our children if we had a cross-party meeting to at least discuss some of our ideas.

The invitation was offered to all with a suggestion that at least each political party send one representative. Out of 111 possible attendees, only one local Councillor, Julien Pritchard (Green Party), accepted and agreed to attend.

None of the other 110 elected leaders even acknowledged the invitation. After a very positive discussion with Cllr Pritchard, ABC sent out a second invitation to all remaining 110 elected leaders… suffice to say once again we received nothing in return from any of them!

Birmingham City Council councillors and elected leaders appeared to be closing ranks and, in the process, turning its back on a campaign to improve the lives of 100,000s of our children living in poverty who needed their help.

March 2020: Covid arrives and coincides with ABC's need to reflect on progress so far and how best to continue progressing the best interests of all children living in Birmingham.

ABC'S EARLY SUCCESSES:

Notwithstanding some of the challenges which ABC faced in its first 2 years... thankfully these were more than compensated for by the great successes we achieved. Here are just a few:

1. ABC organised Birmingham's 1st ever National Children's Day celebration.

    This was a wonderful day where we had two stalls in the city centre simply celebrating all of our children. We gave out lots of free goodies and best wishes. The

local Salvation Army choir's children particularly enjoyed the handfuls of sweets available!

Cllrs Kate Booth and Lou Robinson came to offer their support which was very well received.

Minute Man Hall Green as usual pulled out all the stops and provided us with banners and stands. One local supporter had a friend in Cadbury's who managed to get us several boxes of sweets and biscuits which went down a storm.

Foyles Book Shop kindly donated several boxes of new books which were left over from World Book Day. The Works Shop provided us with a discount on the toys we gave away. John Lewis & Partners created a whole play area in their Bull Ring children's department where staff dressed up in costumes and organised painting workshops and the store tannoy operator kept giving regular shout-outs to customers and about the importance of celebrating National Children's Day. All of these donations came about by just going into the shops and talking to staff who instantly saw the benefit of what ABC were celebrating... no convincing was necessary.

During the day ABC gave out hundreds of pounds' worth of books, gifts, toys, sweets to local children. We also asked parents to complete a petition asking the council to celebrate future National Children's Days.

Overall, the day demonstrated that there is an untold vast well of positiveness towards our children which is yet untapped by Birmingham City Council.

2. ABC began a simple, much overdue and unifying discussion about why all children living in Birmingham

should have their best interests promoted regardless of where they lived or who they were. Not once in two years did we ever hear any one person or organisation disagree with this position.

3. We believe ABC have begun to change the political conversation and context of how all children living within Birmingham should be recognised, valued and nurtured by the whole city. ABC lay down a marker to politicians and city leaders of all sorts that clearly states that all children matter, regardless of class, gender, ethnicity, ability, belief system... if you are aged under 18, then you are one of Birmingham's children and you matter to all of us.

4. ABC had begun the process of challenging all elected leaders regularly to explicitly explain what they have done and what they are going to do to promote the best interests of all children living in Birmingham, not just children in their own constituency.

    Whilst politicians' engagement so far has been less than hoped for, ABC have at least raised the expectation amongst them that they are elected to serve all people, including children in the Birmingham community, not just people in their own constituency area.

5. ABC have challenged the mindset of many local politicians who continue to think and act as though the wellbeing of children is 'somebody else's responsibility'. Many local councillors seem to think that unless you are the cabinet member responsible for children, then the well-being of all children within the city is not a subject they should be concerned about, unless it relates directly to a child of one of

their constituents. This approach not only places unrealistic expectations on one councillor, but it also provides an excuse for other councillors not to act.

6. ABC took the opportunity to raise with a number of local councillors the Preston Model of Community Investment[33] (previously referred to). Given the significance of this recently much-heralded approach by the Local Government Association to building local community re-investment we were surprised that none of the councillors we spoke with were aware of this approach towards managing local government re investment. "The most recent (June 2020) analysis shows that an extra £74 million spend has been retained in Preston and £200 million extra in Lancashire".[34]

7. For a significant period of time ABC provided all 111 local elected representatives and key city leaders with monthly updates on progress across the city. ABC also produced separate ideas leaflets for all councillors and local businesses.

8. ABC demonstrated how easy it is to get like-minded people from various organisations together to sit around a table to discuss how to make Birmingham a better city for all children. In many ways this was a no-brainer; who would refuse? Like many things in life, it was simply a question of finding time to sit down with people and asking them to at least be part of the conversation.

9. The ideas we were discussing and ambitions we wanted to achieve actually cost nothing or very little.

---

33   Preston Model: www.preston.gov.uk/article/1339
34   www.local.gov.uk/case-studies/inclusive-economies-preston-city-councils-approach-community-wealth-building

Most of our suggested changes were cost-free (see the Moving Forwards chapter) and very easy to sign up to.

10. Professional organisations, business and unions were all very keen on being part of ABC campaign to improve the best interests of all children living in Birmingham (Greater Birmingham Chamber of Commerce, National Education Union, Social Work Union, British Association of Social Workers, etc). For similar and different reasons, each of these groups could see the moral, political and business benefit to a community where all children living in it were thriving.

11. ABC ran a 6-month advertising / awareness-raising campaign in the Greater Birmingham Chamber of Commerce monthly publication 'LinkedIn' which focused on the fact that it 'costs nothing to make a big difference' when it comes to promoting the best interests of all children living in Birmingham and other communities.

12. ABC have floated the idea of a citywide children's festival which could be hosted centrally based in the grounds of the city centre universities, Millennium Point, Think Take and Birmingham Conservatoire. This would be a brilliant inclusive use of Birmingham's resources and a showcase for how child-centred the city is. Furthermore, as many cities due to Covid 19 are rethinking their use of city offices into residential accommodation, there has never been a better time to rethink how we might better utilise many of the buildings within the city. In addition, such celebrations could also be staged as satellite events in other parts of the city.

13. Over a relatively short time, ABC had built up an

active and growing following on Twitter, Facebook and LinkedIn where we were able to float ideas and discuss various thoughts with others around Birmingham and the world.

14. We received some very positive local radio coverage (Birmingham Free Radio / Bluedot Radio) and national and international media coverage from as far away as Sweden and Japan.

15. ABC was set up to raise awareness and promote positive change, not to provide services or funds.[35] However, with the limited funds at our disposal we have continued to support a few adhoc initiatives, including the 'Brum Xmas Dinner' which provides a Christmas community dinner and gifts to former Birmingham looked-after children, three local food banks and gifts for many young people who have left the care of Birmingham Local Authority.

16. ABC were also very keen to publicly recognise those organisations which were explicitly doing things, however big or small, that were clearly promoting the

---

35 ABC has a policy of never asking Birmingham City Council for any money in recognition of its perilous financial affairs.

best interests of all children living in Birmingham and in doing so help model what a genuine responsible community-focused organisation is like to others. We were therefore delighted to present awards such as the following to:

Eddie O'Hara presenting an award to staff at
John Lewis & Partners for their wholehearted engagement
with Birmingham's 1st National Children's Day.

Joanne Osmond (ABC Trustee) presenting an award to
Tiger Lab Network Birmingham City University.

ABC also presented awards to:

- 3PB Barristers Chambers
- Aston University
- Foyles Bookshop
- Hall Green Minute Man Press
- Parkfield Community School
- @YoungtrepreneursYCE

In response to ABC giving out much-deserved awards, we also received some lovely photos / letters of appreciation, not least a wonderful photo from a great group of young people at @YoungtrepreneursYCE below.

YoungtrepreneursYCE Youth Group
based in Balsall Heath.

THE POLITICAL RESISTANCE ABC ENCOUNTERED:

"No one is more hated than he who speaks the truth."[36]

Plato

It turns out that Plato knew a thing or two about power!

Given that not one person or organisation has ever privately or publicly explicitly disagreed or challenged the benefit of ABC's aspirations for all children living in Birmingham it does seem almost counter-intuitive that it has received so little local public / political / media support.

Indeed, every politician and senior city manager we have ever spoken to has privately appeared to be very positive about what we hope to achieve, and yet with very limited exception, for the most part, none of them has ever gone public with their support or offered any meaningful assistance and or support. When I asked my brother, Liam, in his role as Deputy Chair of ABC, to meet with two local MPs to promote ABC's aims, he noted that: "Both times I walked out feeling flat and inferior, due to their zero warmth, empathy and understanding."

I've always found hidden / implicit / darker side / softer side of resistance harder to identify and challenge… it's the kind of implied engagement which smiles at you and offers reassurance and then does nothing or the complete opposite. In the world of social work, we refer to this as 'false compliance'. In the world of politics it's known as 'kicking the can down the road'.

---

36   Plato: 427-437 BC.

In fact, 95% plus of elected representatives, senior city managers and mainstream media have simply ignored our 1000s of efforts to contact them… even when a few others have encouraged them to do so.

It came as no surprise therefore that on 1-1-2022 when the local mainstream media were listing and celebrating the achievements of local people recognised in the Queen's New Year's Honours list, that myself and ABC were nowhere to be found… it's almost as though we don't exist!

I continue to find it incredible that a new statutory service with a new directorate such as Birmingham Children's Trust (BCT) displayed such animosity towards ABC to the point where amongst other things, all of a sudden, my job became redundant. And how in doing so they failed to grasp the mutually beneficial role which BCT could and should have played alongside any organisation promoting the best interests of all children living in Birmingham.

It is very tempting to spend a long time describing the above phenomenon and unpicking its various causes, but for the purposes of brevity, I would suggest the main reasons are:

1. For the main part, politicians do not like, some even detest, being held to account for their inaction over important issues. Private feedback from a few local politicians has been that the 'other' politicians absolutely hated our **'Positive Action Report'** initiative which published what our 111 elected representatives had done in the last 6 months and what they intended on doing in the next 6 months to positively promote the best interests of all children living in Birmingham.

2. Most local politicians appear to hide behind a convention which they say means they can only comment upon issues which affect their constituency or ward and then only if the person contacting them is one of their constituents. This protocol provides most of our local politicians with a very a good excuse to avoid engagement on a range of citywide issues and working with each other.

3. Most local politicians still seem to think that anything concerning children is someone else's responsibility and not theirs. This is despite that for any elected public representative, their first civic duty is to serve all of the people in the constituency and broader community. I might be wrong, but I have never heard any politician on election night in their acceptance speak utter the words: "Please be aware that I only represent those of my constituents who are aged 18 and over!"

4. It would appear as though certain local politicians have very clearly put the squeeze on many senior managers of Birmingham's public services not to engage with ABC. It is no coincidence that many of the public corporate strategic bodies are all staffed by the same senior city managers who are accountable to and dependent on local politicians for their fixed term contracts to be extended. With many of our city's senior managers earning between £100-200,000 per year and a new City CEO with a salary range between £186,000 and £227,000 per year,[37] it is not difficult to see whose tune they dance to.

---

37 Birmingham City Council Pay Policy 2020-2021. Unbelievably a few years ago one of our City Council CEOs had an annual pay package of £850,000!

5. The reasons for this are very clear, sadly many of our elected representatives:

   » Clearly believe that 32-54% of our children living in poverty is acceptable.

   » Have limited aspirations for the future of 100,000s of our children or simply don't care. How could they, if judged by their inaction?

   » Are overwhelmed with the complex task of governing our city.

   » Think in terms of short political election cycles rather than the lifelong experiences of our children.

   » Seem averse to talking / working with people in their own party, let alone engaging with others in any genuine cross-party work.[38]

   » One only has to attend a ward, constituency or full council meeting to see how council business functions like a small version of the House of Commons, where rules, protocol, procedure and petty point-scoring appears to dominate any opportunity to have a mature, informed and positive debate / discussion about the city's most pressing issues.

6. Within the above in mind, one could be forgiven for thinking that politically there is no hope. Yet one only

---

38 Some years ago, with my Chair of Birmingham and Solihull BASW hat on, I convened a local summit of Birmingham politicians and the then director of Birmingham's Social Services to discuss the impact of austerity upon children's services. What became very clear was that many councillors rarely, if ever, had meetings with their own party MPs, let cross party meetings. In effect most of the local politicians operated in local political silos even within their own parties.

has to dig a little beneath the surface to find that most politicians and members of our community are kind, caring and want to improve the lives of others. The problem is the current system and culture of petty squabbles and empire-building prevents them from achieving these collective goals.

7. In so far as many of the local public bodies are concerned, despite most doing a very good job with ever-decreasing resources, many still:

    »   Have very low aspirations of what should be done, concentrating on what they can do for fear of being seen to fail.

    »   Some organisations appear to prioritise adherence to regulatory targets (CQC, Ofsted, etc.) rather than be guided by their professional codes of ethics (BMA, BASW, SWE, etc.).

    »   Compete, rather than cooperate or inadvertently delegate responsibility to other public and voluntary agencies to plug the gaps in statutory services.

    »   Provide councillors with filtered information about what they have done, rather than what they haven't done and what needs to be done. It is simply staggering how uninformed many elected representatives are about the services and lack of services which the council does and does not provide.

    »   Spend too much time on rebranding old approaches as the next best thing. When in reality quite often they are not doing anything new but simply relaunching a policy / practice / pilot which had previously been ditched for lack of funding / change of political leadership.

» Blame previous leaders for what is happening now.

» Are managed by a public-service elite who frequently move around the country from one high-paid job to the other. I have lost count of how many new CEOs Birmingham has had over recent years, all promising long-term commitment to our city only to fly off the next post as soon as something else better paid comes along.

» We do not appear to invest in and promote local people committed to our city. Instead, politicians often appoint people who do not live in Birmingham and have no real investment and connection to the people who do live here.

» Local public transport services such as Centro hide behind their regional coverage responsibilities. Despite countless requests to meet with representatives from Centro to discuss the introduction of Free / Reduced transport for children and young people, Centro steadfastly refused to meet with us.

» Operate in silos with a dominant culture of 'this is how we have always done it' and are averse to any idea of doing things differently.

Was it not Einstein who said?

"Insanity is the continued belief that by doing the same thing over and over again you will get a different outcome."

There is therefore now an urgency to change the culture of our city and how we live so that we and our children can all thrive together. As JFK noted:

"There's never a wrong time to do the right thing."

THE LESSONS LEARNT:

"We must talk about poverty because people insulated by their own comfort lose sight of it."
Dorothy Day[39]

1. For many children, Birmingham is a great place to be brought up and live as a child. For many children Birmingham has almost every leisure, academic, social, cultural facility and opportunity a child could wish for.

   Yet at the same time a growing number of children living in Birmingham have no access to these things and simply exist until adulthood, where the future looks bleak for them and their future children. This is not inevitable... poverty is a political choice that our politicians and business leaders continue to make.

2. Birmingham is a rich city and getting richer every day. However, the gap between the rich and poor continues to grow larger day by day. One only has to look at the 500% increase in use of foodbanks in Birmingham.

3. The extent and acceptance of extreme poverty and the total indifference shown by many of those in power across our city is utterly shameful and deeply disturbing.

4. We completely accept and recognise that being a public figure is far from easy, often very difficult and undervalued. We appreciate the good people who step up and step forward to take on this difficult role.

---

39   Dorothy Day, American Social Activist: 1897-1980.

However, we cannot ignore that for those in positions of political power the Local Government Association,[40] on the advice of the Nolan Committee,[41] set out the Nolan Principles which should be reflected by all publicly elected officials.

They are: 1) Selflessness, 2) Integrity, 3) Objectivity, 4) Accountability, 5) Openness, 6) Honesty and 7) Leadership.

On the basis of ABC's experience so far, in my opinion it would appear that some of Birmingham's elected representatives struggle with being accountable and actively involved in reducing the barriers which significant numbers of children in Birmingham face such as: poverty, poor housing, lack of community resources, etc. The fact that Birmingham is such a big council (the biggest in the UK) allows space for individual and collective accountability to avoid the changes which are needed.

5. Statutory services provided by the local council and subcontracted trust (Children's Trust) have been so decimated by central government cuts (60+% over recent years) that nowadays most statutory services are failing to meet even their legal minimum of services. In the words of two local statutory social care leaders, 'our system is inadequate and not fit for function'. The consequence of this is that 1000s of our local 'children in need'[42] receive no additional help

40 www.local.gov.uk/our-support/councillor-development/new-councillor-hub/councillors-role-0

41 Standards in Public Life (1997).

42 As defined by section 17 of the 1989 Children Act.

and support at all. Therefore, for anyone to expect or hope that these institutions will provide leadership and vision for all children across the city is naïve.

6. That the Preston Model of Community Wealth Building[43] re local re-investment is simple, effective and has been shown to save local councils and business millions by local sustainable investment. This alone would massively offset any additional costs involved making any community and / or city more child- and family-friendly for all.

7. In order for children and adults to attain full political human rights, they must first secure educational, economic, social and cultural capital on which to build. Expecting under-resourced and over-stretched schools alone to be the main vehicle for any community to promote equal opportunities and children's rights is a cruel myth perpetuated by ill-informed policy makers and politicians alike.

8. Birmingham Council House is already weighed down by expensive consultant and management reports of what should happen, what will happen in the future, how poor it is in engaging with young people, etc. Official reports, statements and pledges are not enough. Action is needed for sustainable change to happen.

9. Birmingham, like every other similar community, is led by a generation of people who for the most part have enjoyed everything the UK post-war social contract and welfare state has had to offer. Free

---

43 www.preston.gov.uk/article/1339/What-is-Preston-Model-

education, health provision, social housing, social care, unemployment benefit and assistance. Yet these very same people have not only now ripped up that social contract and privatised great swathes of these much-needed services, but they have also accepted the inequality and poverty which comes along with it and made it the new norm.

They have forgotten the simple reason why the welfare state was created in the first place and that was simply because privatisation and pursuit of self-interest alone is no way to create a content and happy society.

10. We have also learnt that whilst there are many decent, principled and hardworking elected politicians, some others are uninformed, self-interested, silo managers and have helped create the mess we are in now, so it is naïve to think, let alone expect them alone to create a different, better society.

11. Birmingham is desperately short on public leadership which promotes the best interest of all. How can anyone regard themselves as a city leader when they focus on what many regard as vanity projects such as hosting the Commonwealth Games / HS2, when in reality, these projects will, as usual, only benefit a few people and not the majority of its residents. The equality trickle-down effect sounds catchy, but in reality, the ever-increasing rise in inequality shows just how much of a hollow myth it is.

12. Birmingham City Council continues to operate a merry-go-round of senior CEOs, directorates and

executive managers who are target-based[44] and come to the city for few years at great expense, rebrand the signs, paperwork and structure, then are lured away for the next better-paid post and leave behind a legacy of resentment and confusion without adding any long-term benefit to the long-term needs of the city as a whole.

13. Some politicians love a good photograph! More than a few local politicians have asked to be photographed by ABC banners for their own promotion, yet never went on to provide any public support for the goals ABC were campaigning for.

14. Local politicians need to regain their strength and throw away the cloak of feeling overwhelmed by central government policy and lead.

15. A Child-Friendly City will never happen until Birmingham as a whole embraces it. The current focus on encouraging schools to sign up to the UNICEF[45] Rights Respecting Schools is in itself better than nothing, but even this tends to exclude those schools who cannot afford to take part in the scheme and in some circumstances does more for the reputation and standing of the school rather than the day-to-day lived experience of a child. Not wanting to sound churlish, but just telling a child they have certain rights without the necessary access to services, culture and food to fulfil those rights, means very little, if anything, to that child's daily lived experience.

---

44 Targets which are generally the minimum statutory levels of services and cost-cutting.

45 www.unicef.org.uk/rights-respecting-schools/

16. Most of Birmingham's 40,000 businesses would be fully supportive of a more child-friendly city that the promotes the best interests of all children. The vast majority of contacts which All Birmingham's Children has had with local businesses have been very positive. Business knows that a healthier, happier, better educated community in the short and long term can only benefit their business.

17. Multi-culturalism is both a strength and challenge which needs to be supported in creating an inclusive, fair and just society for all. There is much to be gained from living, growing up and working with people of all cultures. However, where some elements of those cultures and belief systems promote exclusiveness, this can promote an introverted and exclusive community mindset which may not actively encourage people to positively engage with all elements of their community. Birmingham has some great examples of integration, but it also suffers some extreme examples of communities living side by side and not as part of one community. Our community and religious leaders need to continue to do more.

18. Our experience has been that some local high-profile celebrities which we have been in contact with (media and academia) are keen to have a photo taken beside our banners but rarely follow up with any meaningful support to promote the goals of our campaign.

19. Identity politics in all its guises (culture, ethnicity, class, gender, sexuality, etc.) can be very inclusive to certain groups of individuals within society. However, they can on occasion also appear exclusive and stifle

the reflection and consideration needed to promote the wider benefits of the whole society.

20. The concept of meritocracy is alive and well in Birmingham as elsewhere in the UK, but sadly it is also flawed. There is much to be said about the virtue of working hard as a means to an end. However not everyone starts off in life from the same point. For many who do work hard, succeed and get rewarded, they may find it difficult to understand that their hard work and success was often accompanied by a range of support, opportunities and a sprinkling of luck which comparatively many children in Birmingham do not have.

The underling subtext of this approach to life is that those who do not 'succeed or achieve' are to blame for their own failings because of their lack of hard work and diligence. This approach may console the conscience of those who achieve and succeed in life, but as a statement of fact it is simply untrue. Hungry and homeless children rarely have the range of support, opportunities or luck others have and yet often go on to work harder throughout their lives with very little to show for it.

21. Resistance takes many forms; one of the most effective in polite society is false compliance. Throughout our work we have frequently met with leaders and council employees who again and again, face to face, have assured us of their support and desire to work in partnership to promote the best interests of all children living in Birmingham. Yet no sooner have we left their company, than they mysteriously become

uncontactable and unavailable and fail to follow through on the actions which they had agreed.

22. Many charities across the city do magnificent work helping those most in need. The services they provide are frequently underfunded, undervalued and fragmented. This much-needed and essential blanket of social care, kindness and compassion is clearly built out of the commitment and courage of a great many people who want to make our city a better place for all to live in.

   However, for many of the reasons already referred to above sadly, many parts of this blanket are now almost threadbare and full of holes.

23. That the use and involvement with social media platforms (Twitter, Facebook, Instagram) can, if one is not careful, become a virtual fool's paradise unless it positively improves the lived experience of children.

MOVING FORWARDS[46]

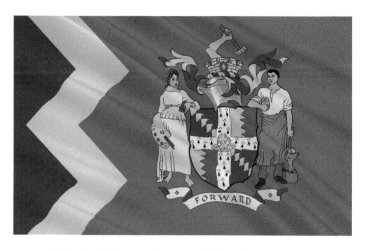

"You don't have to have it all figured out to move
forward, just take the next step."[47]

Having agreed by now (I hope!) that only a section of children
living in Birmingham enjoy the many benefits which our city
has to offer, this chapter will positively look at the proactive
(and often relatively cost-free) and easily achievable ways
in which the gap of inequality between our children could
be reduced and in doing so make a great stride forward in
making Birmingham once again a great city.

---

46   Birmingham City Official Coat of Arms.

47   Anon.

It has always been a mystery to me why Birmingham, as the biggest city of children, our children and how we value them has not been our biggest asset to showcase our city. It's a bit like being the home of the Eiffel Tower or Taj Mahal and covering it in a blanket for no one to see.

The following list of ideas is not an exhaustive list by any standard and many have already been shared with all of Birmingham's elected representatives, many local business leaders and most senior city managers. What is however a prerequisite to considering all of the following recommended actions, is an acknowledgement that to date, we as a city have failed many of our children and continue to do so, and in order to genuinely address this, we now need to have a burning desire to do things differently, want to genuinely value childhood across our city and be part of that change.

Therefore, the focus of this section is not about the better management of people and existing budgets and provision of minimum statutory services... it is about public-service leadership creating a better child-friendly city community where other communities will want to follow.

As noted by Great Thunberg.[48]

"I have learnt you are never too small to make a difference."

QUICK FREE WINS:

1. Birmingham City Council should promote a city culture reflected in the well-known African proverb that:

   "It takes a village to raise a child."

   It could begin this process today by flying the Birmingham community flag from the Council House and other civic buildings, especially as the flag was designed by two local 10-year-old boys, referred to above.

2. We all need to think big – think different – think children, especially our elected business and community leaders.

3. Birmingham City Council should pass a motion and create a citywide policy that promotes and values our children in all that we do.

4. Every single new Birmingham City Council policy should demonstrate how it has considered the impact upon children and wherever possible seek to promote the interests of all children living within the city.

---

48   18-year-old Swedish Environmental Activist.

5. Birmingham City Council should develop a Child-Friendly City culture.

6. Birmingham City Council should begin the process of also becoming a 'Learning City'.[49] This genuinely international approach has already been successfully adopted by Glasgow and Bristol.

7. All new Birmingham City Council procurement and commissioning contracts should be written to create preferred status for those who contribute to the best interest of all local children.

8. Birmingham City Council should use all avenues at its disposal to herald this new approach towards promoting the best interests of all children living in and visiting Birmingham.

9. Birmingham City Council should ensure that any body, agency or organisation receiving any financial support or contracts from the city should demonstrate how they are also promoting, however big or small, the needs of all children living in the city.

10. Birmingham City Council has to start welcoming and be open to learn from its citizens, other communities and cities. We have much to learn from cities such as

---

49 http://lcn.pascalobservatory.org/

Leeds (child-friendly culture) and Glasgow (financial inclusion officers in schools).

11. In line with the Preston Model of Local Wealth Development (referred to above), Birmingham City Council should ensure that all new procurement and commissioning contracts should be written to create preferred status for those who contribute to the best interests of all local children. Over a very short time this will save the council millions and have a profound positive affect on local culture.

As recently noted by Cllr Jamie Jamieson: **"As we look to the future. We should end the emphasis on devolution deals designed by Whitehall and instead ensure that all councils can support new infrastructure investment, join up public services, and provide greater access to jobs and security."**[50]

12. Birmingham City Council should work in partnership with the University of Birmingham[51] to encourage the faculty responsible for the newly created MSC in Poverty, Inequality & Development, to monitor, review and publish the progress Birmingham City as a whole is making towards genuinely addressing the growing inequality amongst children living in the city.

From such a wealthy institution this would be a small, but valuable contribution to the community it has benefited from for over 140 years. It would also

---

50   Cllr James Jamieson, Chair of the Local Government Association. New Statemen: Levelling up Post Covid, May 2021.

51   In 2019-2020, the university recorded an income of £¾ billion which resulted in a £65 million surplus. Value for money statement – University finances and undergraduate student fees – University of Birmingham.

be in line with the beliefs of the institution's founder, Joseph Chamberlain, who established the University of Birmingham to educate and empower those who could not afford private education.

13. Birmingham City Council should work in partnership with Birmingham Medical School, local teaching hospitals and partners, to develop and provide each new baby born in our city with a Birmingham Passport which would set out what they can expect from the Birmingham Community as they develop. This could start by building upon the various First 1000 Days publications which have been around for over a decade highlighting the importance of every child's first 1000 days from conception.

14. Birmingham City Council should implement advertising and educational campaigns promoting the value of children in Birmingham, celebrating our children's everyday lives and focusing on unifying themes of equality, inclusion, tolerance, self-esteem, confidence and joy. One quick step forward would be to encourage all existing digital street advertisers to run positive public-service information to support children, i.e. every day 5-10 second adverts per hour (more if possible).

15. Birmingham City Council needs to run training sessions for all councillors about the make up and needs of children citywide, highlighting how much good the council can do if it works together in partnership with each other. The training should also highlight their legal statutory and general moral duties to all children. Nowhere in the Children Act 1989 or any subsequent supplementary legislation does it say

that children's best interest, are only 'paramount if they are a certain, age, colour, gender, class, etc.

16. Birmingham City Council should ensure that any charities, agencies and stakeholders it works with demonstrate how they are working in partnership with others and benefit all children within the community.

17. Birmingham City Council needs to be brave in telling its managers (CEOs, Directorates and Executive Managers) what the city needs and what they want done. Not wait for the managers to tell them what they can and cannot do.

18. Birmingham City Council should use every opportunity during the Commonwealth Games (2022) to highlight to the world the importance of its huge population of children.

19. Birmingham City Council needs to ensure that all local children have FREE access to at least one event at the Commonwealth Games.

20. Birmingham City Council should work with local businesses to develop a Child-Friendly Charter Mark for any company (40,000 plus) or stakeholder that promotes the best interests of all children in its work / activities.

After a short period of time any company / stakeholder wanting to tender for Birmingham City Council-funded work should have the charter mark. For companies from outside Birmingham wanting a contract from Birmingham City Council, there is nothing stopping them from doing some local community groundwork beforehand. This would be a perfect promotional opportunity for local businesses to be associated with and fund this.

21. Birmingham City Council needs to review its pay structure for senior managers and include payback clauses if any senior manager resigns before the end of their contract which should be at least 5 years. This would encourage senior managers to be part of long-term positive local change.

22. Birmingham City Council needs to embrace the annual celebration of National Children's Day. For a council who supports national Pride Day, the Velo, St Patrick's Day and various religious festivals... the one unifying city celebration should be children, which cuts across all cultures, class, religion, etc. For example:

    Aston University campus, Birmingham City University campus, Mathew Boulton College campus, Millennium Point, Think Tank Birmingham Science Museum, Ulster University, University College Birmingham, Birmingham Conservatoire, Birmingham Ormiston Academy, Eastside City Park, King Solomon International Business School, Birmingham Children's Hospital, South and City College Birmingham, to name a few, are all based in the city centre around Jennens Road... how brilliant and fantastic would it be to close the road and create a children's festival? ABC tried to do it last year but as 'kitchen table'[52] outfit we failed... but with the might of Birmingham City Council in partnership with sponsors we could easily do it. Imagine how many children would remember the day they had FREE ice cream?

23. Birmingham City elected representatives should try

---

52   As described by Andrew Mitchel, MP.

and notify their local media at least once a month about the positive things which their local youth are doing, are involved in and what is available for youths in the local area.

24. Birmingham City elected officials should visit all schools in their constituency and engage with young people.

25. Birmingham businesses should be encouraged to get involved with all sorts of activities, from offering workplace experiences to funding local, parenting classes, etc.

26. Birmingham's local media, press, television, online and radio have a huge role to play in transforming the culture of the city in how they cover children and young people. Rather than continually pushing a negative narrative about children and young people, they need to seriously stand back and take a good long hard look at their editorial priorities so that they don't however unintentionally feed the negative image of many of our children.

Longer-Term Wins at Minimal Costs. (Many of these costs will be offset by additional local re-investment and a reduction in health, social care and criminal behaviour costs.)

27. Birmingham City Council should follow the lead of Glasgow, who have recently introduced financial inclusion officers (as part of their Financial Inclusion Strategy 2020-2025) within all state schools. This will both help families take up the millions of pounds in unclaimed benefits and also help increase the funding per child in schools. It's a win-win-forward thinking strategy.

28. Birmingham City Council and Centro Travel should work together to provide similar levels of free public transport for children that are on offer in other cities such as London, Paris and Manchester.

29. Birmingham City Council should work with the big supermarkets to help fund free school meals for all school-aged children. Did you know that Finland have been providing free daily nutritious meals to all school-aged children since 1948 and they rank as one of the highest achievers for child education? Hungry children cannot learn.

30. Birmingham City Council planners should ensure that any future city centre developments reflect the increasing residential and family nature of the city and incorporate designated free child play areas, as can be found in other cities such as Manchester, Brighton, London, Sheffield, etc.

31. We would invite the West Midlands Lieutenancy to do all within its powers to support Birmingham's civic, community and business leaders to help promote the best interests of all children living in Birmingham.

32. Birmingham City Council should develop a pledge to all of our children that they are our city's jewels in its crown of 1000 trades.

This above list of recommendations is limited only by our imagination in terms of what can be achieved. But as ever, the longest journey always begins with one step **FORWARD**, a word which is, after all, our city's official motto!

SUMMARY AND CONCLUSION

In the early days of All Birmingham's Children's campaign, I met a well-respected local youth activist, who, with a group of like-minded young people, had been pushing for Birmingham to be a better place for young people to grow up in.

They had the ear of many key city stakeholders, 1000s of social media followers and had been given a number of high-profile platforms to promote their work. And yet, despite all of this exposure, they felt after 10 years as if nothing had really gotten any better; if anything, it had gotten worse because in their view the people with power simply didn't care about anyone but themselves and their own families.

Whether or not this is true is in many ways academic; the important part is that for many young people they believe and experience it to be true... for this reason, if no other, it has to stop and stop now.

First and foremost, all children should be valued and cherished for simply being what they are; children are not some kind of mini adult simply waiting for the time to pass so that they can become grown-up adults and start working. Until we recognise and accept this, then we will forever keep thinking about our children and young people as 'incomplete' adults rather than 'complete' children and young people who all deserve to be valued and accepted for who they are. We are the adults; they are the children.

Secondly, one cannot begin to start solving the challenges highlighted above until we as a city (you and me) accept that as a multi-culturally diverse community we continue to fail significant numbers of our own children and that we all have a moral, political and legal duty to do something about it.

Birmingham is no longer the great second city of yesteryear; how can it be with so many of our children suffering on a daily basis?

How can we claim to be a great city when the pool of services, help and support available to those children who are most in need and meet the legal criteria to receive minimum statutory services is almost empty?

If we do recognise and accept the above, then it is never too late to change so that once again Birmingham could become a great city and showcase a new civic role model to other communities across the country in how one goes about valuing not just the selected few, but all of its children.

Once we can accept the above, then Birmingham as the second city is ideally placed to do something positive about it: we have record numbers of children, an enterprising and creative voluntary sector, business community and statutory services and a number of growing faith communities... we just need our communities to collectively raise their expectations of our political leadership to work together for the common good and our leaders to raise their aspirations of what this city can provide for all of our children.

Similar to the approach taken across the world to address the Covid pandemic, the message is that no one is deemed to be safe until we are all safe. The same approach needs to be taken with our children, in so far as none of them can fulfil their potential whilst so many endure hunger, hardship and poverty of expectation and aspiration on a daily basis.

All Birmingham's Children therefore call upon and invite Birmingham City Councillors, Birmingham Members of Parliament, Regional Mayor, civic, faith, business and community leaders to reflect on the contents of this book and then host a public meeting to launch its own action plan on how to achieve many of the recommendations highlighted above.

For our part, All Birmingham's Children will continue to play the role of critical friend and support to Birmingham's political, business and community leaders and do whatever we can to help move forward any new positive plans which promote the best interests of all children living in Birmingham.

Finally, I would like to once again thank HRH the Queen and others for recognising the positive contribution which those involved in ABC have and continue to make to the lives of all children living in Birmingham.

Thank you.
Eddie O'Hara BEM

Footnote: Free complimentary copies of this book will be given within a month of publication to:

- 100 Birmingham Councillors.
- 10 Birmingham Members of Parliament.
- 1 West Midlands Regional Mayor.
- 75+ Birmingham business, community, media, education and faith leaders.
- Countless other national leaders across the city.

ABOUT THE AUTHOR

Eddie O'Hara has been a registered social worker since 1989 and is also a qualified primary teacher.

Eddie currently manages a charitable family support service which supports schools from South Oxfordshire throughout the West Midlands up to North Staffordshire. Alongside this, Eddie provides a range of specialist child protection and adult safeguarding training to Aquarius, Anawim Birmingham Women's Centre, GamCare, various police forces across the North and East of England, the National Crime Agency and British Transport Police.

Over the years Eddie has worked for a variety of educational and social care agencies, including UNICEF, SSAFA, across the UK and from as far afield as Ireland, California, Turkey and Russia.

Eddie was the founding Chair of Birmingham & Solihull Branch of the British Association of Social Workers. During his time as Chair, Eddie always took any opportunity to speak about and promote the best interests of all children living in Birmingham and across the UK, whether that was as guest speaker at the National Social Work Awards or twice as a guest speaker at various national events at the Houses of Westminster.

Until June 2019, Eddie worked as senior manager in Birmingham Children's Trust.

Eddie O'Hara BEM
MBASW, RSW, BA (Hons), SPA, CQSW,
PGCE (Primary), AASW, PQPT, PQCP
www.eddieohara.com